Praise for 7

"Mitzy Sky writes about her Jamaican background with love and honesty, and bares her truths and shares her troubling yet illuminating experiences with the mental health system in America. Her road to healing through examining her family history and forgiveness is a beautiful and empowering journey, and I pray it inspires more women who are going through their own personal troubles, to remind us that we are not alone ~ we are all worthy to be Loved."

—Ishle Yi Parks
Former Poet Laureate of Queens, NY
Winner of the PEN America Award

"Mitzy Sky's heartfelt poetry takes you on a journey of, hurt, forgiveness, healing and redemption. This collection serves as a powerful tool for personal transformation and self-love."

—James Mapes, President
The James Mapes Organization
TEDx, Best-Selling Author:
Quantum Leap Thinking & *IMAGINE THAT!*
Contributor *The Huffington Post* & The Good Men Project
Winner: 2018 Milbourne Christopher Award
for excellence in mentalism.

"It's a beautiful thing to watch an Artist grow, but when that Artist has the courage to mine the deepest, darkest regions of their pain and tribulations; face the ghost and dragons, hiding in the fog of childhood memories with self-truth, it inspires beyond words. Mitzy Sky is this kind of Artist, her poetry eradicates that fog and brings the memories into the light. She explores the subjects we Caribbean people, no talk bout in front ah stranjah. She offers up her own journey through mental health, 'one of our most revered taboos' as a case study in self-love."

—Iyaba Ibo Mandingo
IyabArts
2022-23 Korry Fellow

"From beginning to end *Top of the Zinc Roof* has helped me; in fact, stilled me, to think and consider the throws of life and what we endure or overcome as human beings. Mitzy Sky gives us an insight into the spectrums of her life, the recognition of the ills of others, and the impact it had on her life from childhood through adulthood to the enlightenment of a determined mature space. The Blessing is to see how her steps are continued to be walked out by God to prosper her and not harm her. The impact of storytelling and the influence it has to deliver another while up on our own roofs!"

—Reverend Ina Alisa Anderson
Playwright, Director & CEO
Emerging Voices Production, LLC

"Mitzy is a true poet who can use the power of the word to illustrate the depth of what it means to be human. From nostalgic memories that bring us closer to home, to vivid expressions of pain endured, this collection of poems paints the portrait of a woman who has, and continues to gain, strength and wisdom from her experiences."

—Kahseim C. Outlaw
Wellness Educator & Author

"There is a place so deep and wide that only those who have touched into the deepest part of their soul can reach. Those who have faced the rawest parts of themselves and not turned away bring the rest of the world a precious gift. Reminding us that the true essence of who we are cannot be tarnished and the full human experience will never fit into a small box of labels and diagnosis. In *Top of the Zinc Roof* Mitzy Sky takes us on a beautiful journey through her writing, bringing light to the full human experience the highs, the lows and everything in between."

—Amber Chavous

"This brave and powerful book is a must-read for anyone looking to understand the effects of generations of oppression on people today. Interwoven with prose extracts from the author's life, her poetic voice gives life to the story of how she changed from being a victim of childhood abuse, to professional attempts to deal with her pain through medications, to an awareness of what she needed to do to change, to finally finding her own way to peace. A warm lilt to the poetry evokes her Jamaican childhood which adds to the overall effect of a person striving to come into her own, and succeeding."

—Gabi Coatsworth
Author of *Love's Journey Home*

Top of the Zinc Roof

Top of the Zinc Roof

Poems Observed from Behind the Veil
With a Glimpse of the Light

MITZY SKY

"Grandma" © 2022
"Under the Mango Tree" © 2014
"Dying Slowly" © 1997
"Another Dying Slowly Poem" © 1997
"If I Could Change" © 1996
"I Know Myself (Start From Here)" © 2005
"I Can Feel Spring Coming" © 1996
"Can't You See Me" © 1996
"Out for a Stroll" © 1996
"Wishy Washy Woman" © 1998
"Strength of a Soldier" © 2006
"I Don't Want to Cry No More" © 1998
"27 Things That I Know" © 2014
"The Duck Poem" © 2016

"Only Human" © 2016
"My Mona Lisa Smile" © 2016
"Emotional or Mental, What's the Difference When Moving Forward?" © 2014
"Little Girl, I See You" © 2014
"In This Moment" © 2019
"This Is My Ode to the Trees" © 2019
"Dear Johnathan, What Did You See?" © 2019
"Who's the Boss?" © 2021
"Channa" © 2022
"Sweet Rain Falling!" © 2022
"Hiding" © 2022
"Earth Schooling, Transmute the Pain to Love" © 2022

ISBN-13: 978-1-949122-23-7 (Paperback)

Front and back cover image by Alois Grundner.
Other images courtesy of https://pixabay.com or https://unsplash.com—artists credited when known.
Cover and interior design by Alison McBain.

True Sky Creatives
P.O. Box 578
Stamford, CT 06904
United States of America

First printing May 2023.
www.fairfieldscribes.com

Dedicated to my grandmother, Beatrice Adora Thomas, affectionately known as Mum.

I AM DEDICATING THIS POETRY book in honor of my grandmother, Beatrice Adora Thomas, who I call Mum. I am grateful that when I practiced forgiveness for my mother, Ruby Diane Gordon-Grant, I got to learn more about my grandma Mum's story. I learned that Mum endured a lot of misfortune but worked hard all her life and found her way through. I share my experience with Mum in my first poem, "Grandma." After many trials and tribulations, I saw my perseverance didn't just happen. I observed it from I was a child, which makes it innate in me.

I owe Mum the gift and love of reciting poetry. My grandma didn't know how to read. Looking back, I see she recited the same Bible verses every night and sang spiritual songs to soothe me to sleep. After reading my poem "In This Moment" at an event, people shared with me that the delivery echoed in the room. That's my grandma always being my first teacher, the person I set the most prominent example from, and who is always a part of me. For that, I owe her immense gratitude.

~ Contents ~

Foreword

THERE IS A PLACE SO deep and wide that only those who have touched into the deepest part of their soul can reach. Those who have faced the rawest parts of themselves and not turned away bring the rest of the world a precious gift. Reminding us that the true essence of who we are cannot be tarnished and the full human experience will never fit into a small box of labels and diagnoses. In *Top of the Zinc Roof,* Mitzy Sky takes us on a beautiful journey through her writing, bringing light to the full human experience, the highs, the lows, and everything in between.

Mitzy started as a passive watcher of her destiny, believing that everyone else had the answers to her life and who she was. Allowing labels to define her and various doctors to tell her medication was the only way to fix her problems. Feeling hopeless and helpless to create the life she truly wanted. A victim to a system that does not yet understand the complexities of the mind-body connection and what true healing means. She has gone from being passive to a leader and woman who, by her very life, inspires others to wake up and do the embodied work of healing. Mitzy has blazed a way for others who desperately want to heal but have fallen into the trappings of diagnosis and medication.

We are living in a time where mental health problems are at an all-time high while, at the same time, prescribed medications designed to treat those challenges are increasingly on the rise. It is something we should all be looking into and questioning. I believe the very health of our society depends on understanding the work that Mitzy shares. We no longer have the luxury to turn away from the fact that what we have been doing does not work. In fact, it is contributing to and creating more challenges and sickness in the world.

Mitzy, through her storytelling, helps bring voice and light not only to her own experience but to the many who have not yet found their voice to share. Showing us there is a better way.

–Amber Chavous

Why Am I Sharing These Poems Now?

LUTHER A. BLACKWELL, JR. SET this poetry book into motion to be published. He asked me to share forty-five minutes of poems during one of his shows and I said yes without thinking it through first. I knew I had plenty of poems, but I had never organized them. I just wrote them when the moment arrived. I shared and published some, and others stayed where I wrote them.

The poems date back from 1996 to the present time, 2023, when this book of poetry is published. In 2010 while recording me documenting myself, Luther said he saw me doing a one-woman show. I was nowhere ready for that endeavor and did not react to his expectation of me well. But while I was putting the poems together for the event, I asked Luther if I could put the poems in a storyline. As I started reading and looking back at the poems, they showed me where they each belong. I witnessed progress and faith that the pain I had experienced was transmuting to love. I saw that it didn't happen in a straight line, but there is always light. I could use even the tiniest little light to light up the darkness. And I see how support is so necessary.

After listening to the recordings of the poems I chose for the event I sent to him, he called to say, "Mitzy, you know what this is?"

I said, "Yes, I know, my one woman show. I was hoping that would be your response when you called me back."

He had a great laugh about it because when he suggested it back in 2010, I asked, "Do you want me to jump off of a bridge?" I did not have the strength and confidence back then to walk on this earth as I have in this moment. I hadn't transmuted the pain. I would have only been dumping pain into the world, but now I have something to give back.

Being able to contribute to humanity is why I write, to transmute the pain, as I said, from fear to love. From shame to presence!

Keep in mind that the poems until 2014, I was going to therapy, accepting "mental illness" diagnosis, and using psychiatric services. I believed the diagnoses that I was labeled with and used them earnestly, often quoting to family and friends that my therapist said this or my psychiatrist said that. I trusted the clinicians in therapist, psychologist, and psychiatrist roles to know what was best for me. Finding my way through such an oppressive experience has been a spiritual journey. I reframed my life experiences to say that my soul knew it wasn't the final destiny for me and tried to reach me through my writing and poems to let me know: I was sleeping through this life and I needed to wake up.

Grandma

I arrived at your doorsteps
I could still see your face
My brother and sister
There by God's amazing grace
We stood like three orphans at your doorway
Clutching each other
Wondering where we were and if we had to stay
My brother Tyson in long pants with a white button-down shirt
Matching purple dresses for sister Andrea and me

Even though she's about six and I'm about three
I met an older brother named Patrick and a cousin Steve
Their clothes old and dirty, their pants turned to skirts
Dirty little boys must have been strange
Why it's still etched in my memory half a century
But I was soon to be just as filthy

We arrived in Augustown

Up on a mountain you lived
Long gone from my grandpa's home in Airy Castle by the sea
Where I played on my paternal grandma's tombstone
Had visions of her as I lie in the sun
But I never met her, as she died long before I had begun
I don't remember where we were coming from
And for a long time I didn't care

I forgot about Airy Castle and all the family left behind
I never questioned why
I think it was the life of a child
I lived in the moment catching butterflies
And looking up to the sky
Or could it have been the Dragon Stout with condensed milk and egg
Given to a child before going to bed
The smell of 100-proof rum Christmas punch still lingers in my head

I lived with you for what seemed like forever
But now I know it was but a few years
Until I was eight
When there was plenty to eat
There was PLENTY and even more treats
When there was nothing, you said lay on your stomach and go to sleep

The moon went down
The sun rose, and the cock crowed
We were entuned with the earth
And the way we lived showed
Mountains rose high
The streams flowed glistening water
Tadpoles swimming
The sun-scorched tar burned bare feet walking to school
Patent leather shoes with barbie socks saved for church on Sundays

Pretty taffeta dresses with crinoline underneath

The winds blew
The rain fell and made calming music on the zinc top roof
How did I forget this and go on living so aloof?
Told I would go to America on a plane
It felt like somewhere distant and strange
But I had no television to influence my brain

My cousin Steve and I ate all the dumplings out of the chicken soup
When we were expecting company
It embarrassed my uncle greatly
My cousin Steve was punished severely

His hand getting chopped with the cutlass
I knew when my turn came
Nothing would escape my faith
My cuteness of shaking my frock tail and stomping my feet were
    wearing off
Uncle Ivan would show no more privileges of leftovers
Going to America and leaving my island of Jamaica couldn't have
come sooner
I used my imagination
To create a picture
The plane would fly up in the sky
Drop me off on the rooftop
I would have escaped the beating coming to me
I would be on the rooftop

And you couldn't catch me, not this day
When you forgave me, I'd come down
And I would say I'm sorry
But the plane took me to a distant land

Never to return
I'd escaped my faith
And in my mind, grandma, you I had forgotten
I spent many decades never thinking of you
Uncle Ivan, Steve, Auntie, Bobbie, or Junior

The people I knew
From my big yard down the lane
To Auntie's big house in Kingston
When I finally saw you
I expressed my anger
I thought it was from my heart
You saw in my face danger
I saw in your eyes concern and love
I know now I'd spent eight years of unforgiveness

Mad at you for sending me away
I thought you punished me for being bad that day
I remember the fury of you spanking me
One time was too much, I felt betrayed
You sent me to the store
And halfway there, you forgot
You thought I had strayed
You kept me in the kitchen, always close to you
I learned you were keeping me safe

I learned how to clean and cook like you
I shined the pots with the ash
I did it so well, and it wasn't for cash
Just being close to you was enough for me
First, I was angry because I wanted to play
Now I cherish the moments
You spanked me that day until you heard my cries

"Mum, you sent me to the store," I repeated in tears
You were remorseful
You held me on your lap and comforted me

But my anger wouldn't forgive you
When you died, I didn't cry
My fury wouldn't let me feel for a stranger
For that, I suffered immensely
Seeking help, I was asked
How do you take care of your children so impressively?
Seeking help because of all the childhood abuse I experienced coming
    to America
How could you abandon me to that fate?

The children bullied me and said to go back to Jamaica on my banana
    boat
It didn't matter that my skin was the same color
They hated me and the days became torture
I went home and had responsibilities that weren't an eight-year-old's
You took care of me, and now I take care of my mother's child
How did it all go so wrong?

But that was the care that they asked me about
Bedtime stories to my children at night
A good bath and comfy bed to sleep in
The question asked
How do you take care of your children so well?
That's when I remembered you
You came back into my mind
All that you did
And all that you still do

Grandma, you're the only woman I could ever remember holding me

You're the only woman I remember ever comforting me
Grandma, I remember your strength
Working hard in the fields cutting down banana stalks from the banana
    tree
Swinging it from your back to the ground
Grandma, when I remembered you
I asked my cousin Bobby
Did you think of me?

He said often
To think that you loved me and never forgot me
It warmed my heart
I released the pain of abandonment
The despair from disconnection
I remember the comfort
From your red pea chicken soup
I still make it today when I want to connect back

Grandma, I remember the care
Of you braiding my hair
I remember the Bible stories
You recited before I lay my head to sleep
I remember the love from your singing Psalms 1, 23, and 100 to me.
Yea, though I walk through the valley of the shadow of death I shall
    fear no evil: for thou art with me; thy rod and thy staff they
    comfort me

I remembered that your love was unconditional
I was lacking nothing
Ten years have passed since you died
And I have you watching over me
Grandma, I remember you loved me dearly
And that's when I cry!

Under The Mango Tree

De likkle duty baggy hungry belly pickney dem in a de yard by
     demselve.
De grandmadda and uncle weh tek care a dem gone fe owas.
Dem nu left nutnuh fe de pickney dem fe eat
De house weh dem live ina stand up pon cinder blocks ahn meck outta
     wood
You cahn se hole in a de wood dem
De rain beat pon dem fe how much years now
Dem look gray like seh dem a-go disintegrate
De likkle hungry pickney dem a fe find food fe dem selve
Wahn big mango tree in a de yard
De pickney dem take wahn big stick ahn fling offa de mango dem
Dem lick dung bout three a de big ripe mango
Dem drop *budung-bum* pon de grung
Dem eat mango unda de mango tree until dem belly full
Dem lay dung pon de grung in a de yard ahn look up in de sky
Dem try fi mek shape outta de clouds dem
Dem se dog ahn cow, mongoose ahn roosta.
Dem laugh ahn talk wid each odda
It seems time was endless
Or there was no time a-tall
Dem stare in a de sky until everyting gu blank, looking wid dem third
     eye
Just nothingness – no land – no trees - no birds – no bees
Just looking
Until dem drop asleep, feeling content ahn peace
Dem wake up tu de smell a dumpling, saltfish, ahn callaloo in a
     coconut rundung season wid onions, fresh thyme, ahn scotch
     bonnet peppa

Dem eat until dem belly full ahn lick dem finga
Dem tell duppy stories pon de veranada
Dem wash de dut off ah dem foot before dem gu a dem bed
Dem grandmada tell dem Bible story ahn full up dem head
Dem neva worry bout wha fe eat tomorrow
De Mango tree nah guh nu weh
Eh deya faheva

(TRANSLATION)
The little hungry-belly kids in the yard by themselves
The grandmother and uncle that take care of them are gone for hours
They leave nothing for the kids to eat
The house that they live in stands up on cinder blocks and is made out
    of wood
You can see holes in the wood
The rain beat on them for how many years now?
They look gray like they are going to disintegrate
The little hungry kids have to find food for themselves
A big mango tree is in the yard
The kids take a stick and fling it after the mango
They hit down about three of the big, ripe mangoes
They drop *budung-bum* on the ground
They eat mangoes under the mango tree until their bellies are full
They lay down on the ground in the yard and look up at the sky
They try to make shapes out of the clouds
They see dog and cow, mongoose and rooster
They laugh and talk with each other
It seems time is endless
Or there is no time at all
They stare in the sky until everything goes blank, looking with their
    third eye
Just nothingness—no land—no trees—no birds—no bees
Just looking

Until they fall asleep, feeling content and peace
They wake up to the smell of dumpling, saltfish, and callaloo in
coconut rundown season with onions, fresh thyme, and scotch
bonnet pepper
They eat until their belly is full and lick their fingers
They tell ghost stories on the veranda
They wash the dirt off their feet before going to bed
Their grandmother tells Bible stories and fills up their heads
They never worry about what to eat tomorrow
The mango tree is not going anywhere
It is here forever!

Dying Slowly

"Why do I live?" The preacher says not to ask why. Everything is God's will. Everything happens for a purpose. "Is there a purpose why I am dying slowly, not wanting to live, watching life pass me by? I know she is there. I am aware of her. Is she aware of me? I want to help her, but I can't help myself." She falls on her knees, like a lady in spirit at a Pentecostal church on Sunday morning. She is not praying to Moses' God, who is a burning bush on top of Mount Sinai. "Why?" Her voice can be heard louder than a howling wolf if only she weren't locked in her closet in the darkness. "Why!" "Why!" "Why!" "Why!" "Why!" Her soul is tormented like the souls in hell that Dante wrote. She is a forgotten child, one who had her own. No mom and dad home to go back to, like those children coming home from college. She has no home. There is no love there. She might have been one of the homeless people living under the bridges in cardboard boxes. Cold-hearted people in that house where she lives. People who ruin a child's body and break her spirit. No hugs and kisses like you see on the Brady Bunch. No thirty-minute solution, no solution at all. No one to talk to in that house, afraid to sleep, someone might climb on top of her, touch her small breast that is just beginning to grow. Who are these people? Father? Brother? Uncle? Mother's new boyfriend? Stick her finger down her throat, hold her head over the toilet, disappear little by little, and die slowly. She will die slowly. She is dying slowly.

Somebody, please help her.

Another Dying Slowly Poem

I'm lost, drowning, dying slowly in my own body
The same body that I created to protect me.
417 pounds; who wants to look at me?
It has turned against me.
It engulfs me in a world of darkness.
Lost? Lost! I am, dying slowly.

I wait for death to control me.
To take me to the place I want to be
In my mind, body, and spirit.
If you tell me death is coming soon
I will try and do all I have to do now.
But why?
Why can't I take control of my mind before death does it for me?

I want to be emancipated from the mental slavery
Prozac, Zoloft, Xanax, Ambien, Trilafon, Seroquel, Perphenazine, and
    Abilify have not freed me.
I want to be strong.
I want to be free.

I look in the mirror today.
I don't recognize myself,
I break into a million little pieces
And then I take a piece of the glass and cut my wrist.
I lie on the floor, pain, agony, bleeding profusely
The life drains out of me quickly
This is quicker than the death I live daily.

I want to be me; I want to be more than people see.
The love, the life inside of me, locked away in that tiny place
Unable to get out, unable to be free.
Father, mother, sister, brother, uncle, auntie, cousin… the oppression
    in society
They all locked me down, tied me up, and I can't find the key

Lines from *Vertigo*
"I don't like living," says Kim Novak.
"Why?" says James Stewart
"Knowing I have to die," says Kim Novak.

Photo by Rachelle Christensen

If I Could Change

If I could change anything about myself,
I would change my procrastinating attitude in life.
I have ideas and plans, dreams and wishes,
And it seems no way to implement them.
I think, most of the time, I am living vicariously
Through my children, or my mind is stuck
In the past or fantasizing about the future.

I know I should live in the now.
I have heard that phrase many times before.
I think, once in a while, I do get to the now.
Like right this instance, I am in the now
As I write these lines.
But how long will it last?
An hour, a day, a week, a month?
Never long enough for me to carry out my dreams.

"I Know Myself" (Start from Here, Wherever You Are!)

"What are you doing laying there? Dreaming again, are you?"

"Making plans."

"Wow, you amaze me, the way you can plan. If there were prizes for planning, you would win."

"You are going to move the furniture around today, buy new curtains, maybe a rug for the floor. You see the picture in your mind. It is beautiful. You are going to feel good in this room. It is going to be pretty."

"Red, yes—red, this time. The kitchen is going to be red this time."

"Your bedroom, you are thinking mostly white. Maybe some flowers."

"You are going to start sleeping in your bed—no more sleeping on the couch. You will take a bath every night, brush your teeth and go to bed early, just like you treat your children. You will feel fantastic at night, well-rested and energetic in the morning. Every day will be a new day."

"You will finally organize your filing cabinet after one year of thinking about it. Oh boy, does time fly."

"You're going to start your writing after you change the furniture around and have the front room for your writing room. You will organize those three boxes filled with writings from over ten years. You will put them in order: the beginning, middle, and end of your story. Then you are going to write. You are going to write maybe just one or two pages per day. The good thing about it is that, before you know it, you will finish what you set out to do."

"Your dreams will come true!"

"You will sit at the tables at the Golden Globes, a seat will be reserved for you at the Academy Awards, and your theme song will be sung at the Grammy's!"

"Wow, you are right. You are amazing!"

"You said you could do it, and you are doing it."

No one knows you better.

Thank God.

Thank life.

Thank love.

Thank all the people who doubt you.

And embrace all the people who encourage you!

I Can Feel Spring Coming

A week ago, on a very cold day, I said out loud,
"I can feel spring coming. It's in the air."
It made me excited inside,
My swagger became firm.

As my feet hit the pavement
My stride became fluent and full of life.
Unlike the previous months, as I slept away the days
And each day ran into the next as if I did not exist.

I am looking forward to the day
When I energetically do my spring cleaning.
Every corner, every crevice, every appliance
Inside and out, I will clean.

And what about my insides?
My insides will be bursting out like the angel rays of sunshine
That peek through the clouds,
And I will feel that I could run a mile breathing in the air,

So fresh, so clean, so satisfying.

Can't You See Me?

Come on, take a closer look.
Don't you know who I am?

Come on, take a closer look.
Doesn't anyone know me?
Why can't you see me?

Come on, take a closer look.
Maybe I don't know who I am.
I sometimes believe I am what you see.
Don't you want to get to know me?

Come on, take a closer look.
I am more than what you see.
Deep inside, I can feel me.
I have so much love inside.
Why can't I set it free?

Come on, take a closer look.
Once I was young and carefree.
Then I got the wind knocked out of me.
They said to speak only when spoken to.
So, I left everything locked inside where you can't look.
Why can't you see me?

Come on, take a closer look.
I no longer want to be what you see.
I want to let my spirit free.
Take those hundred pounds off of me.

Would you see me then?

Come on, take a closer look.
Sit down with me.
Get to know who I am.
You cannot find me in a storybook.
You cannot find me with one look.
The love inside of me is more than they took.
Can you feel me?

Come on, take a closer look.
The sweet rain that falls on the zinc rooftop.
The river that runs in the wild.
The fresh air that blows outside.
The rainforest that we need to survive.
The heart that beats, which we need to stay alive.
The love that we feel inside.
I am more than what you push aside.
Come on, can't you see me now?

Out For a Stroll

Yesterday, July 28, 1996
As I walked, I saw you laughing at me.
Before, I asked if you could see me, now I know you can't.
You don't know who I am.
I am sick and tired of feeling like how you see me.
I no longer want to live with this shame.
I tried to show my frustration; I wore it on me.
I am a thousand times more frustrated than your little laughter can
     make me feel.

Girl with the belly button pierced, walking
Holding onto your boyfriend,
Wasn't it enough to know that I don't have that in my life?
Couldn't you have been satisfied inside?
Did you have to whisper and make crude remarks?
When I see you, I know that you are pretty and sexy and dress good,
Don't you know I wish I could?
I wish you the best,
You do not wear your frustration in the size of your dress.

Mister, Hey Mister,
Driving real fast in your car,
Shouting obscenities to me as I stroll on by.
Did you want to see me cry?
Not in this lifetime. I am worth more to me than you will ever see.
Do you know who I know and where I have been?
You can't see it from this fat hanging off my chin.
Would you be happy if I stayed in my house and didn't walk on these
     streets?

Is it your streets?
There are so many good people out there to meet.
I will walk. I will walk these two feet.
You can't stop me.
You don't know me.
I am not just what you see. I have so much more inside of me.
I will set it free.

I came home, and I told my little girl
About the fate I had just met out on the cruel, cruel street.
She hugged me and said, "Mom, I love you."
You see, I am more to her than I ever knew I could be.
Do I deserve such love, such unconditional love?
I say, "Yes, I do." I give it, and I get it back in return.

See lady driving in your car, looking at me with those sad, sad eyes.
Don't feel sorry for me, don't shed a tear.
Cry not for me.
I am more than what you see.

Wishy-Washy Woman

I am tired of surviving, begging, instead of living.
I am tired of being the wishy-washy woman.
I am constantly defending myself and apologizing to you.
Why can't you see me?
I am my grandmother's child, and she would have starved to death
    before she begged for anything.
I am not angry.
You have never seen me angry.

You don't know me well.
You don't know me at all.
Why you would take just a mere expression of my opinion as anger.
Should I not speak?
Should I not express myself?
Should I allow you to continue to judge me?

You're going to think what you want anyway, but I know who I am.
I am the product of my grandmother Mum's love, her mother before
    that, her mother before that, and her mother before that.
I see the light.

I fed you what you needed for years.
Like when I was angry with my mother, you ate it all up.
You couldn't see me without asking, "How is your mother?" As if you
    cared.
And when I responded negatively, you ran back to that square hole
    you live under: "You hear what Mitzy said about her mother?"
I know she couldn't or didn't know how to love me.
She abandoned me long before I came to America,

But at least she showed me that the square hole you live under is hell.
I strive for better.

I am the one that you love to have at your parties, because with me
    there you could be the best thing.
"How you get so fat?"
"Where you get fat going?"
Knowing damn well you hope that I stay that way so that you could
    continue to shine.
With me down, you could be up.
But if that is all you have, you have nothing.
I could fix my teeth or lose weight; hell, I could have my breasts done
    on an installment plan. But what I have gained in here (her heart)
    you could never take away.

You call it mad because I go to therapy to overcome the negative in
    my life as a child, but I see it as strong, not weak.
To make sure my children never suffer as I did, and if they do just a
    little or a lot, they will know how to help themselves.
I am building a strong foundation that will last generations to come.
You know, if you focus long enough on the thing you hate, you will
    become it.

Twenty years,
Twenty years of built-up frustration, sadness, and loss.
You can't see that.
Emptiness, loneliness, wanting, longing, needing.
Needing to be loved, needing to live.

I am tired of feeling guilty,
Guilty about eating, guilty about my color, guilty for living.
I am tired of dying slowly, watching life pass me by, reacting instead
    of living.

I deserve to live.
I deserve to live.
I will live now!

Strength of a Soldier

by Ace Patterson
(Written around
2004-2006)

MY SON DREW THIS PICTURE when he was around five to six years old between 1994-1996 after watching the movie *Free Willy*. He was a natural artist and he always had a story to go along with his drawings. When he couldn't write, I wrote out the stories that he told me about his stick figures, starting around three years old. We had experienced homelessness in 1995, and one of the times at the homeless shelter, he recited a scene from *Snow White and The Seven Dwarfs* to make me laugh. When he asked me if I was going to cry, I told him that I was actually happy. The homelessness wasn't making me sad—I was looking forward to a fresh start.

This is me in the picture, holding up the water, the red door of the home he was dreaming of, his little brother and him on the right, and his sister on the left. He loved *101 Dalmatians* and Michael Jackson, hence the white t-shirts, red shirt, and black pants. The sun is shining as we remained faithful through the hard times.

This poem, "Strength of a Soldier," he wrote about ten years after the *Free Willy* drawing. I asked him to draw a cover for what I thought would be my first book and I told him what I wanted the cover to mean. He also wrote this poem and an analysis.

The eighth summer's sun shined down on the land.
This instant, the innocent should know what time it was.
The girl gazed at the sun from the garden
Envisioning the destiny that dawned upon her.
Her grandmother drifts from the darkness into the daylight
With gloom, gazed at her watered gems, the grandmother
Released a life-altering message while collecting the child's clothes.
It wasn't long before the child was sentenced to a one-way trip to
    travel.
Away she left, and abroad she went; Jamaica was the backdrop.
When the sun moved three times, the girl's toes touched new soil.
There was no light on this new land.
The girl rode the black limousine into darkness, leaving her past
    behind.
For the next ten winters, days were demonically traumatizing:
Neglect, no organization, no loving country.
No love near.
Just misery and malevolence.
The Alighted Soldier turned to her father again and again
To find misery's antidote.
And after all the seasons of anti-affection,
There was freedom on the tips of her follicles
When she walked out the door to follow the destined path.

Analytical Analysis by Ace Patterson:

THE LAY IS ABOUT MY mom and her childhood. Until she was eight, she lived mostly with her grandmother because her mom moved to New York, so my great grandmother took extra care of my mom and her siblings. Once my mom turned eight, her mom called my great grandmother to send all of the children to New York to live with her husband and her. So, after my mom left her beloved country, Jamaica, she spent the next ten years in hell, basically. She went through abuse, malevolence, and ignorance; however, when the time came for her to leave, she left. She built up enough strength over the years to leave the horrible past behind and follow God's footsteps, using his path like a guide in order to live peacefully and free. I chose this story because I feel like I get my mental strength from my mother. Even though she went through depression, she hung on for dear life, never gave up, and to this day, is striving to do better.

I Don't Want to Cry No More (A Song)

I don't want to cry no more
Mother, Mother—I don't want to cry no more
Mother, Mother—Why did you treat me that mean
Father, Father—Where were you today
Brother, Brother—Why did you act that way
Sister, Sister—I'm sorry for all the hurt and pain

I was just a child, a little baby
I needed you to comfort me
But you punished me, neglected me, 'nough brutality
You never talked to me so that I could see
What was going on, what was going on, what was going on

Mother, Mother—Why did you treat me that mean
Father, Father—You were supposed to protect me
Brother, Brother—Why did you die that way
My Sister, Sister—You went, and you did the same

All my hopes and dreams, they went away
Only hate and fear live here today
Joy and Love never came my way
Loneliness filled my days,
Emptiness captured my nights
You abandoned me
There is a vacancy in my heart
Through the witness of, of my eyes
Everyone can see the loneliness inside of me
I don't wanna cry, I don't want to cry, I don't wanna cry, don't want to
    cry no more

Oh why, Oh why, Oh why, Oh why did you go away
I needed you, I needed you, everyone can see the loneliness inside of
    me
I don't wanna cry, don't wanna cry, don't want to cry no more

Mother, Mother—I don't expect for you to change
So, I will change myself.
Father, Father—You were supposed to protect me,
But I will protect myself.
Brother, Brother—After all that you put me through,
Still, I will forgive you.
My Sister, Sister—I will always love you.

I won't cry no more, I won't cry no more, I won't cry no more, I won't
    cry no more
No more loneliness, no more loneliness, no more loneliness inside of
    me
I am free, yes, I am free, I am free, yes, I am free.
No more loneliness inside, inside of me—I, I am free.

I WROTE "I DON'T WANT to Cry No More" in my last semester at
Housatonic Community College in 1998. It was during the first theater
class for the play our class wrote, called *Colors of the Heart*. I had the
privilege to sing this throughout the play after people said their lines. It
was a fantastic experience and one that my children got to experience
with me—their mom from the couch to the stage.

I once performed this song for my sister at her house in Maryland
during her graduation party from Bowie State University. My nieces,
nephews, sisters, stepmother, and dad were there. I honestly was so

caught up in my mind, I never thought about what my dad would feel at that moment or if this affected anyone around me. I heard whispers that he was displeased, but no one said anything to me. I don't think people knew how to speak with me then because I was pretty much convinced I knew everything. Unlike now, where I know nothing but know I can learn, I understand and respect others' worldview. These days, I practice hard to be still and listen to others.

27 Things That I Know

1. I learned to trust white people before I trusted Black people because the Black people in my family first abused and misused me. Then I went to school, and the Black kids bullied me. I loved learning, and I only had white teachers who taught me. Until Mr. Tinkler showed the kids at Mckinley School that a Black man could care about them. He would greet us in the morning at the school entrance and talk with us to show that he genuinely cared for us. In the beginning, I didn't understand what he was doing. I don't even remember who the principle before him was. I was shy and held my head down, but he kept talking and saying good morning every day. I can recall the moment when I looked up at him and opened my mouth and said, "Good morning, Mr. Tinkler." He smiled at me and the connection happened. I was confident that he saw me.

2. At eight years old coming to America, I did not get messages from society to love the people that look like me, therefore I couldn't love myself. I had to unlearn the hate toward myself and stop the judgment of "less than" that I was unconsciously learning.

3. Trauma caused by physical, sexual, and emotional abuse, lacking, abandonment, and loss hindered my growth and progress.

4. Shame is what I was dying from that caused so much suffering.

5. Anger and aggression come from shame. Anger works better to move forward from adversity than sadness. However, as the Bible says, in your anger do not sin. Which means for me do not hurt anyone or yourself. Know that anger is an emotion that you can express and doesn't have to be you. All your emotions are valuable.

6. Learning where the pain comes from has set me on a path of gaining awareness.

7. Feeling joy for others did not come easily in this lifetime. The message of "better than" is what I learned, and it seems to cast a lot of judgment. Judging others means that there will always be someone else better than me, and that does not work for wellness because the grass is never greener on the other side. Everyone is going through something.

8. Learning to let go of judgment and "better than" helps me to feel joy for others' success and not feel "less than" or left out.

9. I know that people who have more than enough are willing to share with me and others.

10. I learn not to judge the people who won't share because they may be experiencing feelings of lacking, and holding on makes them feel like they are winning. They are afraid of others winning. I've learned that it is not material things that make you win. It is power in your awareness and compassion that is more than enough.

11. Belonging, love, connection, and practicing forgiveness are what I need, not labels in the form of diagnoses and drugs.

12. Practicing forgiveness helps me to let go of pain, even if it comes with a good cry, and then allows me to feel joy when needed to move forward with love.

13. Love is much better than Fear. Fear controls; it is not love.

14. Love, trust, faith in the present moment that is where you find God.

15. Shame resilience is the best thing to practice. It started from the Bible; he who hasn't sinned cast the first stone.

16. I am learning that God is Love and that some Bible stories created to control cause harm. Unlearning helps me to stop moving in fear, and instead choose love more often than choosing fear. Therefore, I stop judging and condemning people and stop judging and criticizing myself.

17. I know that the wisdom God has given me has touched many others. I can see and feel our presence together. I give the glory to God, and I keep learning and sharing.

18. I know that I don't want what belongs to anyone else because what God has given me is more than enough.

19. Giving God the glory and knowing there is something greater than myself keeps me humble.

20. Respecting all life and God's creation gives me peace.

21. Trusting my child at three years old to say to me, "Mommy, I will tie my shoelaces at four," gave him space to be free and to trust me and to trust each other.

22. I know I could get weary in giving when I don't get back but keep going, and this too shall pass until I get to a place of giving without expectations when joy comes from within.

23. I know that the ones who I give to will not always be the ones who give back to me, so I keep giving.

24. I know that I sometimes feel that I have given way less than what I have received. I'm learning to receive wholeheartedly; therefore, I'm giving back wholeheartedly.

25. I know that the blessings I have received are way more than I could have ever dreamt.

26. I know that the gifts I have received are because I have learned to forgive, which has allowed me to receive.

27. I use my imagination and see the life I lived before in my mind's eye. I feel that I returned before because I didn't learn what I needed to learn when I was here. and I pray that I have become conscious of it and will not need to return. I know this is the one life to live on Earth.

The Duck Poem

I won't be writing any more dirty poems
I can't do friend me, fuck me, and leave me
I discovered I'm way too aware for your shit
Alive, living in the moment
Too free for that shit

I see through lies, and I'm asking for honesty
It doesn't matter who you are; your name isn't important
There are enough of you doing shit to make this poem relevant
There is enough women like myself looking for love and pleasure
Getting caught up in pain, trying to measure
Up to that first touch
Thinking I missed you so much
Scratch that, not labeling myself, this was a moment of distraction
I want to thank you
I paid attention
Found out what lessons I had to learn
I just gained some confidence about this game
I'm good—cocky, no, because I'm worthy—that's why
Your game just got a little better to increase the score
You ain't never met someone like me before
You told me it was your birthday in September
But now your friends are celebrating you on social media in November
I'm going to have men on rotation that I could call and who will give
    me attention each time I meet a new one; it will always be my
    birthday
So money will keep coming my way
Fuck it, the pussy is going back on the shelf
Lock the chastity belt

I don't have daddy pain issues
Forgiveness is a gift
You should try that, my friend
Otherwise, what sense does it all make in the end?

I won't be writing any more dirty poems
I can't do friend me, fuck me, and leave me
I discovered I'm way too much aware for your shit
Alive, living in the moment
Too free for that shit

I want to thank you for the lessons learned as I get my head back in the
    game
Fool me once, I don't live in shame
Did you expect to see me broken and maimed?
I think you enjoy causing women pain
I tell you, I give freely, and that scares you
Because you need someone you could hurt and deceive, and I just
    wasn't the one

I won't be writing any more dirty poems
I discovered I'm too aware for your shit
Alive, living in the moment, too free for that shit

Tupac warned us not to build a generation of babies that will hate the
    ladies
He asked, Why do we rape our women?
Do we hate our women?
What does this hate look like?
Womanizing
Leaving a young mother to care for the baby by herself
Poverty is a bitch and a significant cause of trauma
Get a job, pay that child support

Don't complain; she shouldn't have to take you to court
Ms. Lauren Hill says that she is only human
That she has been through the same predicament
Every time I think I'm enlightened, some shit happens
That grounds my ass back to show me that I know nothing
This is my duck poem.
I'm just shaking shit off
I chose to be better than myself yesterday, not better than anyone else
I compete against myself
I won't bring this negative shit into the next relationship
I'm shaking it off; you should try it

I won't be writing any more dirty poems
I'm too aware for this shit
Too alive living in the moment, too free for your shit

Too many hurt men
Insecure men
Lost men
Ex-girlfriend pain men
Mommy issue men
You are not allowed to hurt me. I didn't hurt you
You gotta deal with your past shit
Face that shame and fear and stop using it to whore
You deserve freedom
You deserve to live well
I said I don't want to comfort your inner child
Only because I been away from that shit
I see your pain; I'm attracted to it
It fuels my inner pain
I want to rock you on my breasts and be your best friend

I'm not writing any more dirty poems

I'm too aware for your shit
Alive, living in the moment, too free for that shit

Dick is coming my way like a rainy day
You underestimated me as a stay-at-home
Now you call me a busybody
I got places to go, things to do, money to make dreams come true
I need you to trust me, even though I see what you do
I never did the same shit you've done with me; accuse me
Because I'm not what you thought I was
Someone to sit at home and wait
Brooding and intruding over you
360, motherfucker
I'm going to need a strong man
Insecure men need not apply
Little boys with mommy issues need not try
I didn't hurt you, and I won't pay for your pain; that is my only reply
Give to me, and I will give you respect beyond your wildest dreams
That's just me

I won't be writing any more dirty poems
I'm too aware for your shit
Alive, living in the moment
Too free for that shit

I need someone who needs me, but I don't need anyone
You need someone who needs you, but you want to fuck everyone
The two of us are so much alike that we don't need each other
We are running from love
You hide out in pussy
I hide out in celibacy
But we are both hiding nonetheless

I won't be writing any more dirty poems
I'm too aware for this shit
Alive, living in the moment
Too free for your shit

Just a temporary distraction, your dick had me caught up and twisted
Your touch had me mesmerized as you used every portion of my body
    to get off with it
More pain than pleasure
The third time was a charm; you came armed
With your skills of pussy managing
You could run a corporation
Sorry for your childhood
No solid foundation
Sorry for slavery
It still got us mentally fucked
You didn't do this to yourself, but you alone can free yourself
Black men, victims of police brutality and senseless deaths
This is not post-traumatic stress you are experiencing
This is oppression continuously
Have to figure out how to help your sister, brother, father, and momma
Have to find ways through sometimes limited resources
How to make your dreams come true
Dropping out of schools, less college enrollment
And more prison cells with 70 percent of Black and Hispanic men
Big prison systems are created and then profit from your predicament
Can't you see the setup?
You gotta wake the fuck up
America found a way for slavery to continue
Thirteenth Amendment said free but not free
But that's not the worst of it,
The thing that we do to ourselves and blame each other
Fucking mental slavery

Photo by Achim Scholty

I won't be writing any more dirty poems
I'm too aware for this shit
Alive, living in the moment
Too free for your shit

Not dissing the Black men
I love Black men
I only see one race
The human race
This happens in every spectrum of the human experience
I just haven't ventured out beyond my color; I'm comfortable with it
But I'm getting curious. I don't see love with color
I see by the content of your character
I'm getting beyond the judging people thing
It's becoming a spiritual thing
I wanna know if I'm feeling your energy
There are lots of Black men fighting for human rights
Respecting the sisters, mothers, and daughters

My sons are Black men
I love how my son treats his fiancée, his wife-to-be his best friend
I raised that man
Giving the glory to God
So many things he could have gotten caught up in
I lived through my friends, cousins, and brother getting gunned down
    in this life
I love the Black men
I want freedom, not just for some but for us all

Did anyone notice I put God in this poem?
There should be no shame in sex for women
The rules made up by men that overpower and discriminate
People's sexual orientation, equal rights and justice for all
Women are not supposed to admit that they like to fuck
I mean, have sex
I mean, get made love to
While little Black girls could get stolen from school, sold, and abused
Children of all races molested by relatives
Told to be good girls, then tossed aside for the next
Growing up locked in mental institutions because they can't free their
    minds from that mess
Drug companies and psychiatry are making millions from that shit
More Black men labeled schizophrenic started after the Civil Rights
    Movement
The label was once reserved for White women who didn't want to
    clean or cook
She said she wanted to party; you called her a bad girl
You want me to be a good girl, then be a good man
I believe in equal rights; let's move past this world of discrimination

I won't be writing any more dirty poems
I'm too aware for this shit

Alive living in the moment, too free for your shit

But yes, there are a lot of curse words in this poem
A little bit of aggression I'm detecting
Anger and aggression come from shame
I'm admitting you fucked me over
Said we could be special friends
Said I could call you when I needed it
I'm not a stalker, one call
No answer, and I'm done
You let me down; the game was over before it even begun
Women do get confused and twisted
But that's because you feed them so much bullshit
Their gift is to nurture and support
Guess I'm on the right track
To wait for the one who could do the same for me
You were never the one
Asking me to live in secret
Get the fuck outta here
My mistake
My bad
I should have never said I wouldn't tell
Obviously, that was a lie
I don't live in secret; I live in freedom
You should try it
Anything less is dying slowly
Choose to live
Life is a gift!

I won't be writing any more dirty poems
I'm too aware for this shit
Alive living in the moment, too free for your *SHIT!*

FORTUNATELY FOR ME, I HAVE found my way out of some severe misery in this life. I feel joy even when happiness comes and goes. But there are people in my life hurting. I meet people every day, caught up in what society says should make us happy and better than others. I hadn't felt pain in a while, so I got curious about someone. Yes, indeed, he brought the pain. Have you ever seen ducks fight? They go at it hard, and then you see them flap their wings and shake it off. Then they go back to swimming beautifully, like nothing ever happened. This poem is my duck poem. I'm shaking off this experience, except the lesson has been worth it.

The lesson learned in 2016 was that I had turned fifty and was afraid of sex. Afraid of men. Fearful of my sexuality. My womanhood was not enough to be seen, heard, and validated as worthy. Afraid of speaking up. I went through the experience thinking that I was aware of life, but found that I was hiding out. Yes, I worked and met many people and many different circumstances, but I didn't venture out of my comfort zone. My last husband before that was my cousin's baby mother's brother. After that, I had a brief sexual relationship with my cousin's brother from his father's side.

I didn't seek to talk with strangers. I ventured out from Bible study on Wednesday nights to open mic every Wednesday in 2016. At first, it was terrifying, but then the creativity and standing on stage all came back to me. It had been two years of being off psychotropic drugs. I faced the fear of what people thought about me, and it allowed me to create and share in a public space.

I wasn't looking for a relationship, nor was the person's role as an intimate partner. I was curious. I decided that I was fifty and I needed to be brave. Emotionally, I felt I had just turned twenty-one. I could now do what I wanted and not care. It was the level of shame that had me tied up about sex. After a time, I came to find out that I was stuck about sex, but I pretty much had way too much awareness to be treated less than I deserved. I couldn't go back to doing one hundred and ten percent while sometimes receiving less than fifty percent. I wrote a dirty poem about degrading myself and read it at the open mic. I know now it was me trying to take my power back, but it didn't give me the strength I have within now from practicing forgiveness and getting to know myself.

After I read the poem, men looked at me strangely and curiously. Their eyes seem to be saying: "You look too strong to be saying shit like that. Are you that weak? Could I do what I want to do to you?" Older men weren't curious enough, but someone half my age was. I was caught still trying to be what I thought I should be in my mind and new to the nightlife scene that I didn't know to ask, "How old are you?" He came to me; I wasn't looking, so we decided to have fun. It wasn't a conscious decision to take the risk at turning fifty. It was something my spirit led me to do, as my soul knew I had reached half a century. I couldn't continue sleeping through life, and dying slowly. I needed to wake up and live. I needed more awareness. I needed to embrace the earth schooling and stop running.

One morning I skipped work, and he spent the morning with me. He sat on the floor in front of me, next to my bed. We were so in tune, just silly, having fun, and talking about our dreams. I had no dread whatsoever. He said to me, "You're like about sixteen in age." He looked in my eyes affectionately. In a whiny voice, like I would have done when I was sixteen, I said, "I'm more like twenty-one." I was owning that it is okay to have sex and not feel shame as I did when I was sixteen and getting molested by older men and couldn't have orgasms with the person who was supposed to be my boyfriend—too caught up in my mind of shame and lacking presence in my body. I got pregnant at seventeen and didn't once have an orgasm with the person I had sex with.

This opportunity to move through shame came, and I took it. He told me his age was less than half my age. We had a few more times of getting together, but I knew it had to end. After almost losing my life smoking a blunt with him laced with something like fentanyl, I ended it. I lay there, feeling my heart speed up and passing out. Something told me to jump up, waking me up a little. I could have panicked and had my heart go faster, but I did what I had learned to center my body. I relaxed and lay still because I knew stillness speaks, even if I was dying. I know now, after having many experiences of the other realm, whether in a dream or a vision, it was someone greater than myself who told me, "Get up," when I sat on that chair and not to drink any wine on that 2016 New Year's Eve that could mix with whatever drug that was in the body. I've learned more over the years to listen to that stillness, but back then, "The Duck Poem" was how I released the pain and returned to the present. I listened to *Pony* by Ginuwine for two weeks straight while writing it. I was all in my feelings. I knew I was getting caught up in wanting to care for someone else and not myself. I wasn't working on writing my book. I worked the nine to five, and then I spent time thinking about the person's creativity. In the beginning, we had talked about our creativity, but now I saw his goodness and was drifting from mine. I needed the strength to take it back. Music works to help me do that when I am writing poetry.

When I read this poem at open mic for the first time, I asked the host to have the DJ play *Pony* when it was my turn to go up. It played, and I walked on the stage with so much confidence. I held the microphone, sang the song, and danced sexy as much as I could at over three hundred and thirty pounds. When I finished reading the poem, the DJ played a reggae dance song loudly, and it vibrated through the building. All the young females in their twenties that I had gotten to know, who were regulars at the Wednesday night open mic, jumped up on the stage to dance with me. We danced and dropped it hot and cock-up bottom and dropped it to the ground. It was a fantastic, validating moment. And so is this poem...

Only Human

Only human
I slipped and let in the pain
Now I'm feeling it
Breathing it
Living it
So much fear
Too many burdens to bear
It seems everyone I love, and people I meet, are hurting, suffering
I lose focus
The pain is staggering
What do I do? I can't keep letting it in
It feels like the enemy will win
Telling me the whole world is born in sin seems like the people will
    continue suffering
We only have this human experience; the pain will come again
But there are things to do to recognize and let go
Live free in the moment as we began
But it hurts so much
Help me, please, this pain is so real
I'm gonna let this go now; this is not how I choose to be
But I see you
Know that you are worthy
There are choices
You could choose to be free from this pain too
You don't have to hurt yourself or anyone else
You could make a choice
Choose love
You ask how
Practice forgiveness

Practice giving back
Practice shame resilience
Practice compassion
Practice empathy
Practice presence
Just never give up
There may be things hindering you that you have to give up
Give them up but don't give up your life
Don't judge people unreasonably
You will judge yourself the same
Wreck yourself the same
What a man thinks about me is none of my business
What I think about myself is everything
Those are some excellent places to start
Then read and learn from others who have been there before you
Let their words validate your own life experiences
You have your inner compass
Stand on the shoulder of giants
Be with people smarter than you
Actually, we all only know what we know
You have so much to give and sow
Keep learning
Never stop learning
When fear comes your way
Be curious and walk through it, choosing love, come what may
You will be amazed your persistence
Will bring resilience
Your perseverance
Will bring resistance
You were not made to crumble, the songwriter writes
Even though sometimes you may stumble
This is a human experience
The race is not for the swift but for the one who endureth

Learn now
Live now
Choose life
Choose freedom
Choose to live
Now

My Mona Lisa Smile

I'm smiling my Mona Lisa smile
as I write this.

I understand why Maya Angelou
writes, "Pretty women wonder
where my secrets lie."

I meet this beautiful woman,
body curvaceous, good job,
beautiful smile, well dressed, hair
done well, and a handsome Black
king for a man on her arm.

She greets me and plays her
games to pretend the man is not
her man, checking to see if I
know him.

The next time we meet in the
same circle, it is her man, and he
is the father of her beautiful
children.

She greets me with "honey" and
"sweetheart."

Terms of endearment or words
used to sting someone you feel
less than you or to make yourself
feel bigger and stronger.

Photo by Mirko Bozzato

I feel so calm inside—on the
outside, there is my Mona Lisa
smile.

I know that it is my strength
inside that you see: perhaps it is
the look in my eyes, the power in
the palm of my hands, the
confidence that I show despite
my noticeable battle scars.

I call my obese body and missing
teeth "battle scars" from
surviving poverty, oppression
under psychiatry.

49

This group of people that I was
labeled to be was not to endure
or be among the living again.

Yet here I stand among the
educated, the artist, the
politician, the affluent. I stand
because my worldview is that we
are all worthy. I know I have a
right to live, and everyone else
does.

Sister friend, I understand why
you would want to misjudge me.
There was a time past I didn't
know myself.

But next time, step to me and get
to know me. Don't judge from
your insecurities, especially
when you walk with the diamond
beautiful Black man.

Here is the thing, I see you. I
know that is your man, and I will
respect you and treat you as I
want to be treated if that were my
man.

Trust me; I know how you feel. I
had a man like that once, but he
did not love himself or me.

I couldn't walk into my house
without the neighborhood
women at the housing project
surrounding my car to speak with
him.

He did not love himself or me.

I walked into the house by
myself and left him to be what he
wanted to be.

I learned it had nothing to do
with me. I'm looking for
connection and kindred spirits.

That means respect is the
minimum.

It matters who you have
surrounding you and your
children. You don't want
someone who will disrespect
you.

Love matters in all forms.

Boundaries are essential to me. It
leaves me free to be me and
respect myself and my sisters to
the end.

Love matters when I love me.

I see you because I see me.

Sister friend, don't let my Mona
Lisa Smile bother you.

I'm just confident of my light
within.

Emotional or Mental, What's the Difference When Moving Forward?

One person accepting a diagnosis, as I once did, said to me, "The mental health services people got it wrong, "I've gotten to know you, and you weren't 'mentally ill.' You had emotional problems."

I said, "Well… the mental health records on me list at least four diagnoses that I know are stored up from seeking help to stop the pain and suffering."

After years of therapy and taking prescribed psychotropic drugs, I remember getting to a place where I started asking to read the files; they had been accumulating on me.

I finally got curious and wanted to know what was going on.

Why was this taking so long?

I was nowhere closer to the American Dream of a white picket fence and Mercedes Benz. Instead, I had become homeless with my children. I got reported to the department of children and family services for not being able to feed my kids properly. Diabetes, arthritis, blood pressure—insulin, cholesterol medications, and acid reflux medication. The obesity got worse as I continued living a sedentary lifestyle, binging and purging.

I didn't know it was because of the frustration and disgust I felt about myself, not learning how to accept the present moment.

Instead, lacking, needing, and wanting were the constant mind occupant.

The therapist I was seeing didn't allow me to touch the files physically. She held the files and handpicked some for me to read.

The powerless feeling I felt back then just arose in memory.

But with that thought, also the thought that the person was doing what they felt right to keep me "safe."

Then my next thought is that the person had no idea of the curiosity I had inside of me.

Why I was asking to see the files was something that she couldn't see. She had agreed to give me the worst labels. Someone she couldn't reach. Someone she couldn't teach. Someone whose light they considered had gone out.

I was waking up. The spark of hope.

There was a time in my life when I would have used the phrase "recovery from mental illness."

What did that look like at that point in my life?

I was on many different prescription drugs, antidepressants, and antipsychotics.

I learned the "mental illness" language, and when I was confident in it, started sharing with others to, "*Stop the stigma so that people can reach out and get the help they need.*"

I had accepted all the labels and thanked the therapist and doctors for the diagnoses and the positive words they started to say toward me.

They noticed that perhaps I wasn't delusional, as they had once judged me to be.

My light was very much inside of me.

It had never gone out, merely God carrying me.

The part of my life that was causing me to move forward was not the labels and the drugging or the people in professional roles seeing me.

I had long let go of that fantasy.

It was the fear of my children following the same path as me.

It was years of moving through what seemed like endless pain and suffering.

I read books, watched people's stories in movies and documentaries, and talked and got to know the people I met.

It was strangers coming into my life and becoming friends, who offered support that didn't judge me less.

They showed my children and me kindness, empathy, and compassion.

My friends came into my life and saw the deteriorated condition I lived in.

They gave us food, a phone, a car, a computer, and decorated the apartment.

Just some basic needs that validated us as worthy indeed.

Then for the first time in over a decade, the therapist I was seeing came to the apartment where I was living to quench her curiosity.

I described and showed her pictures of the generous gifts.

That Oprah moment, "You get one, you get one." I got one, and it took an angel's heart!

I was confident that I was moving forward with my life circumstances.

I started taking risks, knowing that I wasn't alone.

To tell you the truth, I've learned the word "compliant."

I would have to say I was compliant being someone's "mental patient."

Looking back, I did every group recommended.

I just wanted to be seen, heard, and validated.

I couldn't say I was compliant with the psychotropic drugs, though.

My sisters almost died of drug overdoses.

My cautiousness about taking drugs had the people in the professional role make me not feel whole.

The drugs with the long, strange names were the scariest.

But I could see now that I couldn't read the name on that drug at eleven years old, which made my sister Andrea go into convulsions.

I couldn't stop my sister Tots from taking my mother's orange-colored blood pressure pill that left her with only a few minutes of her life to live.

I once returned a shopping bag filled with pills to the mental health center.

Perhaps that's why they started doing bloodwork to check the level of their drugs in my system.

I started taking them because they gave me one with a shorter name that I saw on a television commercial. It made promises of feeling energetic and getting back to doing things outside that would make me happy.

But even that pill couldn't keep its promise

It didn't address the adversities that I went through.

It didn't address the spirit that wanted to rise to its soul.

My moving forward was the fact that I never gave up.

I kept meeting people who sowed a kind word or shared with me their life experiences of living up to or striving or thriving for their best human potential.

My moving forward was truth that let me feel the emotional pain about the abuse that happened to me in childhood.

I cried many tears to let it go, and then I started to forgive the people who harmed me.

I also forgave myself for the hurt I caused to others and myself.

My moving forward was that I remembered the things that caused joy.

I had not talked about it while focusing on the shameful things that caused pain.

It was the fact that forgiveness helped me to remember my worth.

Forgiveness removed the veil and gave me back my confidence.

Forgiveness helped me get back my awareness.

I can walk with my head held high, knowing I have dignity innately, as any other person having this human experience.

My grandmother taught me how to give when she had me give up my bed to my cousins, and I slept on the floor.

Yes, we were dirt poor!

But joy doesn't have a price tag.

It's all coming from within.

We just have to open our hearts' doors!

Emotional or mental, what's the difference when moving forward?

Someone categorizing my reaction and behaviors to suffering has nothing to do with the chemistry makeup of my DNA.

The injustices in the world seem to be here to stay.

I used to scream or stay in silence, asking, "Why me?"

I've learned that from you treating me as a victim.

To live an inferior existence is not shame on me.

My power I must take back immediately!

Accepting all my emotions, no wishing, hoping, and pondering.

Knowing life is suffering, and this too shall pass.

What I think about myself and knowing my worth

It is that I deserve dignity from birth!

Little Girl, I See You

Little girl sitting on your grandma's lap
I see you
I see all that I want for you now
What you could not see for yourself
I want you to have all that you need and desire
I want you to have dreams and goals and work hard to accomplish
them
I want you to grow up and feel your body, mind, and spirit as one
I don't want you to separate your mind from your body because of
pain and shame.
Little girl, I see you going to school
Learning, connecting, and creating
I see you learning about the world and its people and respecting
everyone
I want to see you play, like you played in the yard, by the stream,
rolled down the hills, hid in the bushes
Little girl, I see you
All grown up, you read, you learn, you travel
You meet beautiful people inside and out
You write, you create, you share
Little girl, I want to tell you
You are going to suffer much abuse and go under much scrutiny
But this will all work for your good
As life/God has set it out to be
Trust that life knows what is happening and will transpire at every
moment
Be flexible
Be courageous
Be fearless

And you will prosper
Forgive the people who caused you harm
Forget about not having anything under the Christmas tree that was
    your first one in America
Life will give you everything you need
Family
Friends
Connections that never end
House
Car
Whatever you may need
Remember no need to look for love
Little girl
You *are* love!
Live in loving awareness!

In This Moment

"Bringing the gifts that my ancestors gave, I am the dream and hopes
of the slave," Maya Angelou writes in a poem.
I could fully embrace that now.
But in times past, when I was a child, lying with my back against the
earth, looking up at the sun, the blue sky around me, awareness of
my being,
I had no connection to that statement at all.
For once upon a time, my ancestors had peace and freedom.
In those moments, that was all I had.
I bear witness that I had to experience psychiatric oppression to
understand the oppression of slavery.

In this moment, **I AM SO SORRY.**

I was compliant, given labels and drugs, saying, "Thank you, more
please."
I was not rebellious like the people who tried to free themselves from
slavery and were labeled Drapetomania. Equivalent in my mind to
forced psychiatry.
People who knew of the injustice and fought for human rights and
freedom.
Instead, shame and guilt consumed me, and my fear was used against
me.
I blamed myself, as the oppressor judged and labeled me.
Colluding with my torturers, saying something was wrong with me.
Instead of asking what happened to me, causing me mental slavery.
Desperate for the "American Dream" shown on TV of Mercedes
Benzes and white picket fences, I accepted the help.

Agreeing with the labels caused me to judge myself the same, and I
 became my worst enemy.
I did not teach myself this hate toward me, but only I could remember
 freedom and free myself.

It is no excuse to stay unconscious and not learn and grow.
The ignorance I thought was bliss almost left me lifeless.
Used for someone else to profit from my suffering.
Drugged, but they called it medicated.
Labeled, but they called it diagnoses.
Hindered, but they called it helping.
Having peace and freedom again in this lifetime is no small thing.
Having peace and freedom again in this lifetime means letting the pain
 in.
Having peace and freedom. Peace and freedom. Peace and freedom
 mean feeling every emotion, perhaps looked at like "sin"—
 sometimes it was.
Having peace and freedom in this lifetime means forgiveness and
 letting love win.
I beg you to remember freedom
As the first existence on this planet called Earth.

In this moment of time, my grandma is getting beaten.
Unable to go to school, not learning how to read.
In this moment, my grandmother is reciting Bible verses to me.
Every night before I lay my head down to sleep.
I am grateful for her great memory.
In this moment, my mother is being raped by her brother
And threatened to be killed by him when she speaks up, asking him to
 stop raping their little sister.
In this moment, my mother is beating me with electric cords and
 rubber hoses, telling me I am black and ugly like my father.

I BELIEVE HER.

In this moment, I see my mother; she is a little girl, and she hasn't
    healed.
She feels pain. She wants to feel love. She hurts, so she wants to hurt
    me.
My peace is a threat to her.
My questioning her inadequacies is a threat to her.
I know she only did to me what was done to her.
In this moment, I work hard for awareness.
My suffering was never a brain disease that any pill could heal.
In this moment, my mind is wrapped up in the hurt and pain, thinking
    of the past, and dreaming of the future that never will come.
The time is always NOW.

In this moment, I buy my mother dinner and sit and share life with
    her.
She is proud of her grandkids.
In this moment, my father has all he needs and more from his parents
    but is taught he is "less than" by his grandfather.
Great granddad said, "Leave the mangoes on the ground, let them
    rot."
My dad was a hungry belly little tot.
A wealthy man with a fancy car once treated him nicely.
The effects of "better than" still lingered greatly.
My father wished to be a big-shot man and drive big cars, have lots
    of money and nice clothes.
In this moment, my father is manipulating his child.
He says, "You should make sure people always like you."
In this moment, he is touching me.
I want him to love me.
In this moment, I have cried many tears, hated myself, think that
I would have been better off dead.

Feelings of shame and guilt consume me.
In this moment, my tiny hand is holding his as we walk in
    the sunshine.

CONFIDENCE IS MINE!

In this moment, I forgive him.
In this moment, I am telling what has happened to me.
In this moment, family members won't speak to me.
In this moment, it doesn't matter if anyone likes me.

KEEPING SECRETS WOULD CAUSE MY SOUL TO DIE.

In this moment, I have children that I desire to love unconditionally.
Instead, I've come to expect them to live for me while I die slowly.
I've created great burdens for them to carry
By dumping my suffering and my sorrows on them.
In this moment, my child tells me that he sits at the closed window in
    the dark with the curtains drawn.
He has watched my loneliness engulf me.
He wants to reach me.
He tells jokes to make me laugh.
He sees me sad and asks, "Mommy will you cry today?"
I don't know how to reach him because I can't reach myself.
I am numb on psychotropic drugs.

In this moment, I accept a diagnosis for my child.
I look to those with titles in their professional roles to tell me what his
    human experience means.
I don't push him to study hard or read a book.
TV has taken over our time to share, talk, learn together, or even cook.
Fast food has become our constant remedy to comfort what cannot be
    comforted.

A hole in the space that should be a mother's and a father's love.

In this moment, my child wishes me to see her.
"Mommy, look, I am standing at the edge of the train track.
Come and catch me before I fall.
Mommy, look, why can't you see me? Don't you love me at all?"
Yes, my love, I see you, but I can't see me. In this moment, I am
    stuck.
You tried to rise above, but my words of failure and defeat kept
    repeating.
Repeating. Repeating.
I tell you that you are the eagle, and there is no bottle.
You can soar as high as you want to fly.
In this moment, you are my child, and I want freedom for you.
Baby girl, can't you see, I went to ask for help.
I dreamt of a better life for you and me.
But accepting the labels left me like a monkey with my hand under the
    glass, reaching for the peanut. Stuck!

COMPLETELY FORGETTING MY GREATNESS!

What was happening in my mind?

Shame, blame, disgust, fear, pain, better than, less than, anger, regret, lacking, burdens.

I wanted to love you, I wanted to love myself, but I kept judging, comparing, and competing.

In this moment, I don't know what love is, for if it is never received, how can it be given?

In this moment, all of us are living in this vulnerable world.

I've learned to respect others' life experiences and take risks to live my own.

Strangers have become friends that support me and lift me up.

Yesterday is gone.

Tomorrow is not here yet.

THE PRESENT MOMENT IS BEAUTIFUL!

In this moment, love has returned.

Who does it profit to call myself names?

In this moment, it makes me feel validated that I wasn't bad for the things I couldn't control that happened to me.

But then the label took away my expectations to live up to my best human potential, and what that meant for me.

In this moment, I start to dream again.

I see myself running as fast as I can again.

I start learning about myself again.

In this moment, others can't see me.

I have to see myself.

In this moment, I ask the question, Who says I'm well?

In this moment, I lose trust in myself, and I ask, How do I know I'm well?

In this moment, I am consciously unlearning all the things I
   unconsciously learned,
And I know that I decide **WHO I AM**.
In this moment, learning to let go as quickly as possible has given me
   the strength to forgive and move forward, not expecting
   perfectionism.
In this moment there *is*... forgiveness.

I've gained awareness... I found myself worthy... in this moment
I find you worthy.
I believe we are all worthy.
In this moment, I want a mother and a father.
I imagine it means unconditional love.
In this moment, I have support, love, connection, and belonging. The
   suffering has brought clarity.

It's not about the pretty.
It's about the **PRESENCE**.

I work to stop letting "pain be motivation."
I am from the kidnapped people sold into chattel slavery.
Their strength used to build nations.
I'm from the people who held their children up to the sky, saying,
"There is nothing greater than you under the sun."
Because of internalized oppression, I'm the one who forgot how to
   have fun.
In this moment, I'm rolling down hills, walking barefoot in the
   streams, and catching butterflies.
I am the hopes and the dreams of my ancestors.
In this moment, I have peace.
In this moment, I am free.
In this moment, I'm just me.

AFTER READING *THE POWER OF NOW* by Eckhart Tolle, this poem came about, and I have been fully embracing it for over five years. Then I experienced the MAHFA written and directed by my friend Ina Anderson. It was such a powerful gaining of awareness and getting into the spirit that Black people's first existence was not slavery and to think of the freedom, the kings, the queens, the families, and the connections that happened before people's human experiences were used up in slavery. Sometime after that, the place where I work had a one-week workshop with two teachers from Kripalu. We did a meditation exercise on the last day, and then we were left to draw and free write. I wrote "In This Moment" during that session. After a while, I continued to develop it and had Ina help me edit it to take out things that weren't needed or repeated. What you read is the final version. It is published in *We Are the Change Makers: Poems Supporting Drop the Disorder,* edited by Jo Watson and published by PCCS Books.

This Is My Ode to The Trees

Little tree standing tall on the corner
Why are your leaves turning brown before the other trees?
Is it because you're older than the other trees?
Is it because you're younger than the other trees?
Has this part of town been colder than other parts of town?
Does the sun not shine where you are often?
Are you in a R-U-SHH for winter to come?
Is it natural for your leaves to turn brown before the other trees?
Time is a thief, isn't it?
It comes and goes, and you don't even know it.
Is it because it doesn't exist?
Until the wrinkles on my face or your empty branches show it
The summer months have come and gone, and here we both are.
I've been watching you consistently.
I noticed when you were just bare branches during the winter months
The sun hitting the snow that fell on you in all the right places.
A beaver could gnaw at you for hours and take you down
But you stand there effortlessly like you don't care.
I noticed in the spring when you started getting your new stride
The dead of winter started to wash off with those April showers
Refreshed and renewed when the first buds began to peep through
You really showed off when your leaves were fully in bloom.
You stand majestically
Rooted deep in the earth and pointed to the sky
You are always looking up, knowing where your strength lies.
But time is a thief, and the months have gone by
Your leaves are turning brown and starting to fall down

The winter months will come again, then spring, then summer, and
   back again.
Your time on Earth is timeless!
I want to thank you for the oxygen you give to me.
I want to thank you for the shade that you offer me.
I want to thank you for the awareness of the stillness of your being.
You stand firm in the rain, snow, sun.
You stand tall in the forest or even desert.
Every tree is different and unique
Your shapes, your colors, your heights, your branches.
I feel blessed to see you!
I know you exist
I know you know I exist
I am grateful that we all exist.
Every moment that we have here on Earth is a blessing
So thankful for the lessons.
I've lain under you and looked up to the sky
I could see the sun glistening through your branches
Sparkles of sun rays, bringing twinkles to the eyes.
You know your worth on this planet
You stand still yet do everything you are meant to do
You exist so that I can exist
I learn from you.
There is nothing I have to do; I could just be free
But if there are things my heart desires to do
Then I learn the lessons, take the steps, and, "Get it done!"
You taught me that the only thing constant is change
And to keep moving forward, I have to learn to grow
But I don't have to know everything.
Stop the judgment of others that defeats oneself
Instead, stay curious and develop learning experiences that bring forth
   insight
Treat others how you want to be treated; giving respect is a minimum.

Dear trees, you're not comparing one to another
You stand tall together, intertwined, judgment-free, and the stillness
    speaks.
This poem has no particular rhyme, but it does have a reason:
Sharing the lesson to look up.
Sharing the lesson to look inside
Before you look outside for your strength.
There is something greater than ourselves
You won't find it in a store on a shelf
It costs nothing, and the gift is priceless
Just feeling grateful for another day
Just doing what I do, being who I be.
This is my ode to the trees.

Dear Johnathan, What Did You See?

I can't write this poem without tears falling from my eyes
It's okay to let the tears roll from your eyes.
I'm writing this poem thinking of you.
I remember the first day that I met you
You bounced down the stairs at work
Then shortly, I learned that you were the new person hired to work on
    the young adult team.
I introduced myself and learned your name
Johnathan
I never dreamt that I would be writing a poem for you
It is an honor and a privilege to sit here and think of you.
Your infectious smile!
Your optimism.
Your intellect.
Your wisdom far beyond your twenty-two years
Even though they consistently electrocuted your brain.
You kept learning and gaining knowledge, all the same.
It is an honor and a privilege to stand here today and read this poem to
    remember you.
I let the tears subside as I wonder… what did you see?
What did you hear?
What brought meaning to you?
I'm so sorry I never got to know too much about you
We learn to give each other space
With the hope that one day we will feel safe
And let all of the secrets out by grace.
No more shame to hide
And you stand up tall when someone speaks your name
Johnathan

I saw you as a blank slate as I once was, with your curiosity,
eagerness, and courage, ready to learn and write on.
I chose to build the relationship slowly, with respect and mutuality.

Johnathan, what did you see?

You learned voraciously and gave back with a giving spirit and a heart
of gold.
Your story will never go untold.
Secrets and lies will all come to unfold.
I listened to you share your stories at the partner's training
I sat quietly
There was one moment that I cried inside
The thought that you endured such treatment in just twenty-two years
of your human experience.
However, there was hope because you found a place that would back
you and support you to reach your best potential.
You went out, and you worked hard for the team.
You met with senators and leaders in all that you could reach.
You wanted to teach them.
You wanted to reach them.
Show them the injustice that happened to you, which is still happening
to so many others.
You worked honestly and passionately, and they all saw you.
But when you spoke, it was quietly.
You showed those who would judge you a threat to their well-being
Though you were innocent, peaceful, kind, and serene.
I often asked you to repeat what you said.
You spoke big words sometimes that I couldn't comprehend.
I wanted to hear you.
I was hoping you would speak louder, but you never raised your voice
any higher.
So, I drew my ear closer, quieted myself, and listened.

Sometimes when I couldn't hear you, I thought perhaps your energy
    was on a higher plane way above mine.
Your final voice was a roar.
Can you hear me now?
Yes, I hear you.

Still, I ask, Johnathan, what did you see?

Did you see them, in the beginning, saying how much they love you?
Did they pinch your cute baby cheeks and show you off to family and
    friends?
Did they give you everything you wanted until they figured the
    cuteness had ended?
Did you have a clueless family thinking the psychiatric system would
    save you?
Did someone hurt you, interrupt your spirit and take confidence from
    your being?
Did you see your body respected, or did they not see you?
When you cried out for help, did they ask why, or did they decide for
    you?
I know you spoke of your young brain electrocuted and your memory
    loss.
Did you see yourself having to rebuild your memory continuously?
No matter how many times you rebuilt it and proved your intelligence.
Did you see yourself locked up as a treatment for your good?
Did you see yourself deciding "never again," no more punishment that
    would continue your suffering?
You stood up and fought for a better way.
You mastered every training that they threw your way.
You started to receive every accolade that they created.
Was it that which doomed your fate?
They hate to see the opposite person speak.
They fear not being seen and heard.

72

They build roadblocks for you to jump over.

Johnathan, what did you see?

Did you see them say that they loved you when you first met them?
Were you not able to know and see their control for power as
　　blindness?
So young, only time would have shown you the truth.
The privilege from fear and shame of not being seen and heard.
Did you watch them give you compliments for the little things that
　　didn't matter?
For the big things that mattered, they turned their backs on you.
Did you see that you wouldn't get the support they give each other to
　　take a break?
To walk away and come back and live another day.
Did you see them take whatever they wanted, even after you built it?
Did you see them walk into the room and pretend that you weren't
　　there?
Did you see them laugh, talk together, and share with themselves and
　　exclude you?
Did you speak up and ask to be seen and heard, but they dismissed
　　you?
Did you see them take the gifts you gave them and then put roadblocks
　　in your way, so they don't have to thank you?
Did you see them treat someone who looks like you well?
To show each other that they didn't hate you.
Trying to make you think the problem was you.
But the fact was they were purposely excluding you?
Did you give them love and compassion and make them feel safe?
Did they turn around and use it to hurt you right in your face?
How did you learn to fear someone with the same color as you?

Johnathan, what did you see?

Did you see the power, the privilege, the money, and the titles that
    keep some happy and leave others suffering?
Did you see the well-oiled machine that keeps on spinning and turning
    and how it is all feeding each other?
Did you see the systems of oppression set up to fear a young Black
    man and leave him helpless?
Did you ask them not to speak for you, and they said you shamed
    them?
Did they tell you that they called someone?
Did that feel like a threat to you as you remembered Emmitt Teale,
Oscar, Philipe, Eric, Sandra Bland, and Trayvon?
Did you see the hypocrisy of someone speaking of love and
    connection but who would blot your light the first moment you
    started shining bright?
Did you see that people are doing what they are doing for themselves,
    and all the titles, power, and privilege they get to keep for
    themselves and even take what belongs to you?

Johnathan, what did you see?

Did you see that working in a system like psychiatry was hopeless
    when you are pathologized?
That the profit goes to the ones who wield the DSM book.
To hear that you had quit.
My thought is: I would never have let you go.
I would say to you, Johnathan, I am not letting you go.
You have given your heart, body, and soul to this work.
It is hard work, but I'm putting an investment in you.
Your gifts that you came to give the world, and this you will
    accomplish.
You have gotten to know the ins and outs of this mental health
    recovery system of work.

Why don't you take a month or six months off and rest?
The journey is long; you have gained so much knowledge and wisdom.
Why don't you take some time to get to know yourself?
You have given so much you have become exhausted.
But don't quit, just rest.
Your cup is empty; you need it filled back up.
It is possible to fill your cup when you are right here on Earth.
You need not leave us yet and go soaring into paradise.
Stay for a while longer.

Johnathan, what did you see?

I shared how I use my tears to release the pain from injustices.
The ones who will profit from saying you died by completing suicide.
They will promote suicide prevention.
But we know the truth whether we want to admit it or not.
You died from a broken heart caused by moral injury.
I heard you say on a podcast that "love hurts"
And you, "Love until it doesn't hurt anymore, and then there is only
     love."
You are in love now, and you have always been in love.
Like a rocket ship, your body came for just twenty-two short years and
     did a lot of heavy lifting.
Like the rocket ship breaks off, leaving all the heavy parts before
     going into the stratosphere, so has your body been left behind.
Your spirit has soared higher and higher, meeting your soul.
The everlasting love!

Johnathan, what are you seeing now?

MY THOUGHT HEARING OF JOHNATHAN'S death was, "So this is what the mental health system breaking your heart feels like." A twenty-two-year-old taking his own life from moral injury. To not get heard, seen, and validated after giving his all. To grow tired and weary when the wheels of injustice that keep on turning get revealed in a place where you were expecting equity, equality, justice, empathy, and compassion. At twenty-two, I wasn't even aware of the mental health system yet. This young man, at twenty-two, had been in it for six years. He shared stories of his mother never visiting him, not once when he was institutionalized in the state psychiatric hospital for five years. How could that be? Something happened to him that he could not speak about, if he was anything like me at that age.

Johnathan's friend and a coworker, who his death affected deeply, asked me to write this poem to share at the memorial service for him. She had received many emails and had numerous conversations with Johnathan about the discrimination and violation he was experiencing.

I wrote this poem, remembering Johnathan and reflecting on what I've seen and experienced working in mental health as a person who once sought help from something I knew nothing about, especially the loss of power. His Holiness, The Dali Llama, said that if you can't help someone, at least don't hurt them. These words that you read off these pages are not meant to cause harm to anyone but simply to bring awareness, as growth happens in the uncomfortable spaces. My intentions are to move forward, looking at how we could build connections and not the competing, comparing, and labeling that separates us.

No one person could be blamed for Johnathan's death. My opinion is blame would further take his voice from him. We live in a multilayered system of oppression, and I have no clue how far the rabbit hole goes. People pretend that they don't know, so if you know, then it is up to you to share. I knew that I had to stop fighting and simply be aware that I didn't know and that perhaps others don't know either. Awareness is a magnificent tool. Once you become aware, you still have the choice to choose fear or love. I have taken some time to look within to see what Johnathan's death has shown me. I noticed that I kept myself small, so he had nothing to look up to from me.

He came out of the state hospital, speaking up about the injustices he endured and what he saw. He spoke to the leaders, senators, heads of agencies, the money, the power, and the titles to ask for help. We consciously and unconsciously learn that these things are what rule the world. He wouldn't have thought to come to me, as I know he saw me in a role with absolutely no power or voice in the environment where we worked or the society in which we live.

I wish I had more time to share with him all I knew. I only had a few moments. Perhaps it was too much awareness to go from what you *think* to see what it *is*. My unconsciously learned internalized oppressed self recognizes to speak up is to make others feel uncomfortable and threatened, and that they say it's dangerous. Johnathan spoke up often, and they pretended to listen to him. He even created, and they took it from him. He was genuinely disappointed. But I wish he knew what I knew at twenty-two, "That success is the best revenge." He could have kept on going. As he matured, he would then have learnd to embrace all his emotions, for that is true success in this human experience—to be in touch with all your emotions as they are happening.

I did try to share with him that awareness is the true strength. And with everything, give God the glory. You could use that to know the truth and work in systems of oppression and not believe what it seems the majority wants you to think is the only way. You get to know yourself and forge your own path, and sooner or later, you will find support from people who also believe that transformation is needed today.

My creativity had me listening to Pop Smoke's song *Dior* for two weeks while writing this poem and thinking of Johnathan. Music seems to help me reach the pain to stay and fight, rather than be sad and flee. I see the vision of Johnathan roaring and soaring through the galaxies. Death can't hold him down.

Who's The Boss?

You gotta teach people how to treat you
Not the easiest thing
People usually have difficulty with me when I teach them
I show them that I'm the boss over what I do
They fuss and fight because they look back to the days when I didn't
	know myself
The days that were great for them
When my talents and gifts were used up
Left me feeling screwed up with no credit or profit
People who use titled roles for their worth have trouble with me being
	the boss of myself
I am the boss, they say to themselves
I say you have a title and a role
There are things you are required to do and lead
Why does that make you full of yourself?
Don't you know yourself?
Everyone deserves dignity and respect
A title shouldn't be the only thing to get that
Who is the boss?
Your great old days aren't so great anymore
Your privilege to take and not earn has got you living in terror
You cry your tears, or you say out loud your titles every time you get a
	chance
You feel insignificant without one
All your pain and sorrows are right in front of you always, and you are
	looking for someone to blame
Half the time, you don't know the task that the team is completing
You hang onto every word that someone with knowledge is speaking
You take it to the people with the titles, and they say that you are smart

You smile and feel satisfied, but inside you are enraged
Because you don't quite know yourself
You feel fake
You need someone to blame
You turn to look at someone else as less, and you say to them, "I'm the
    boss"
You feel lost
You have a title
You have a role
You have some tasks to do
Some places to go, some people to see
Respect is earned
You are not the boss of me
I lead my destiny
I see what needs to get done, and I get it done
It is my responsibility to know my purpose and still do work
My worth is not tied up in the task of making money in the land of
    milk and honey
That wants my head bowed low, and my back bent
Giving some a false sense of security and superiority
I chop the wood, and I carry the water, and it is just what it is
Getting this work done, transmute the pain, and gain awareness
A word from Ram Dass,
"We're all just walking each other home!"
It doesn't matter if you're living in a castle
Under a bridge, in a cave, in a mansion, on an estate, or in the hood
Connection within, you are still good
Support without judgment is necessary
I shouldn't have to stand next to you for my worth
I deserve dignity from my birth
When it's manipulated and stolen
It won't be giving back
You have to take it

Forgiveness with empathy, kindness, and compassion will get that
   done
Who's the boss?
You know how to lead with equity, dignity, empathy, and compassion,
   and you have the skills to know what the whole team is working on
You see the goals, you do your part, and you delegate to others
You take the time to take care of yourself.
Your cup is full and running over, and your passion, kindness, and
   wisdom shine through
You know your worth and, in that awareness, you know that everyone
   else is worthy
You value the people, and your moral compass uplifts their spirits
They complete their task, and the whole team shines
You know when to promote because someone else's success doesn't
   make you less
Who's the boss?
You're the boss!
Listen, the next time you step to me, know this
I will still give you all the knowledge you need from me
It may elevate you still to the positions you desire
Know this: it doesn't make me inferior, whatever your thoughts are
   about me
You thinking that you are clever and using me
You still need wisdom and compassion to be free
Until you rectify what you have done, your suffering will continue to
   be
Know this for sure when you step to me
I am not your negro or your mental patient.
I will not be shrinking to fit today.
You make this look easy
Writing flowing out of me, vomiting up the disgust you try to spew on
   me with your words of disease because you are trying not to see
   me

You want to be the boss
What does being a boss mean to you?
I no longer think you know everything
I see through your tricks of taking what you want and leaving debris
    behind
When I asked for what I needed to do the job
You said I changed
Casting the blame of your insecurities on me
My god, I used to beg you to see me
Asking, why can't you see me?
But now I know I need to see myself
Lately, I've been feeling myself
But I see you pimping, setting up roadblocks with privilege, ignorance,
    money, policies, procedures, and policing to keep your foot on my
    neck
You owning your title and keeping it as your worth; that is your right
You taking it to mean disrespect and inferior treatment
You are showing people the misconceptions of feeling insignificant
The need for someone to be less, for another to feel great
That is fake
You cause moral injury
But it doesn't matter to you; to see someone else hurting for you, it's a
    win
I couldn't pen this thing if I didn't know its origin
Been there, I've done it
This is all judgment
I see me. I see you; why I'm making all these comments
I'm still a giver; it's apparent
You keep coming to me to take when you are in a drought
Nothing new to share from your own thoughts to give you clout
To the people who count to you
We all want the same thing, to be seen and heard
When status and titles are for your worth

It doesn't matter your gender, ethnicity, or color
You will always choose the status quo
Validated by the majority and money flows
But what is it to gain the whole world at the cost of your soul?
The money isn't real
What a thing to say
Shout out to the people who take a second look!
You are the change-makers
You stand tall, heads high, and face all the naysayers
Who's this woman standing here now before you?
I done unlearned the bullshit
Here I am. I got a glimpse, and my perspective done shift
I've been beautifully created. Perfectly imperfect
Knowing where my strength lies
I see your fear; you're afraid to be found out, caught out. But let that
    go
You only know what you know
Set yourself free from pretending
No, you can't have my creativity; you have your own
No, I don't have any money; that's never what you wanted
It's that freedom in my spirit
The rise in my back
That confidence in my walk
That smile in my eye
That wisdom behind the veil
So, you used that shame that kept it there
How are you, a boss?
Do you care about me or just about you?
Did you really go there?
Asking me to use language influenced by the DSM
To move backward for profit to big up yourself
You use it, and so you want me to use it too

Don't you see because of the color of your skin or economic
    background, you are seen
You get sympathy, and you think you can win
I tried that, and it almost did me in
Labels and drugs left a poor girl dreamin'
Left to die slowly in poverty with no expectation from my beginning
    to end
Here is a little gift from me to you
That took me decades to learn
Twenty-twenty said learn it now
Or continue with your dreams deferred
"Focusing on all the negativity
Blocks the creativity."
It's like playing football, and I'm always on defense
Not getting to play the offense to move forward
Less will be yours when you chose love over fear.
I will not receive accolades from those who promote "mental illness,"
    healing, and recovery.
I'm sticking to what I know for sure.
Life happens, and sometimes it is suffering.
A word from Viktor Frankl, *It's my job to find meaning in the
    suffering.*
I heard DMX r-o-a-r this sentiment.
I glimpsed the truth and kept on letting the lessons unfold.
Allowing me to gain wisdom that's worth more than silver or gold.
A word from James Baldwin, "Perhaps the turning point in one's life
    is realizing that to be treated like a victim is not necessarily to
    become one."
This one here. Just in case. One more time.
I am not your negro or mental patient.
I will not be shrinking to fit today.
Who's the boss?
What does a boss mean?

I get to know myself
Captain of my ship
Observer of my thoughts
I decide my actions
I make my choice
Next time, you step to me
Remember, you're no boss of me
Momma being calling
Now I'm walking in my destiny!

Channna

Dearest Channa
I write poems to transmute the pain to love
I find it strange to be writing to you now that you have ascended above
You never waited for your turn to let your light shine bright
During your short time here, you learned to be the light
You gave so much to others
You knew your strength
You were fierce, caring, and showed kindness and compassion
You did not live with your emotions caged
You even understood the power of rage
It showed in how you lived, laughed, and loved
You must feel all your emotions to stay in touch with your spirit, body,
    mind, and soul

Channa, I'm writing this poem for you
Because I'm seeing you through my mind's eye
Baby pictures
Toddler features
Teenager, adulthood
And the role of your son's first teacher, preacher, and goddess of pure
    love
You excelled in all the things you set out to do
You had love from a family that will never forget you
It is fitting that we come here today in bright yellows and whites to
    celebrate you
We took the opportunity once to sit down and converse
We talked about you being created beautifully by God
Who sets the universe and guides your footsteps
Not for men to judge

Because only the One knows your heart
And only the One directs your path
I asked what kind of things you would like to do with this human
    experience you were having so authentically
You shared the hard work that you did taking care of others with less
    ability
You shared your goals of becoming an entrepreneur
Your spirit lit up when you said it was to take care of your family
And make all your dreams come true
I thought how selfless
So many in their twenties only think of themselves
But you were from another breed
One that consciously raises their seed
Your mommy, sissy, BJ's daddy, and all your family will make sure
    your son continues to succeed
You're from another level
People that give to not only their beloved family but also to their
    friends
Including them and celebrating with numerous birthdays and holiday
    traditions
There was never any doubt how much they cared
Your beautiful baby boy
You dreamt bigger for him than others would, dear
You respected his spirit so he can rise to his own capabilities
But you not only dreamt
You put your knowledge and work to the test
You spent time teaching him and training him to run in the sand to
    build the strength in his legs
A future Olympian, you said
You spent time reading him books and teaching him
That he could get the best education
Some people dream
But you worked to make the things you saw a reality

Channa, I'm sitting here writing this poem for you
I know your body did the hard work while you were here
Like a rocket ship taking off
You have dropped the body, and your soul is soaring higher and higher
in eternity
With our Heavenly Father, you will remain until we see you again
You stuck around as long as you could
You fought hard from the beginning of the news, and we cheered you
on
Fight, girl, fight
The thoughts that some may have is that you lost your battle with
cancer
But for those who have been paying attention in this earth schooling
You took off a tight pair of shoes and a suit you wore exceptionally
well for thirty-two years
You dropped the body that we became accustomed to in this earthly
realm
But your light will shine forever more
There is no end
Through your family
Through your legacy
Through your baby boy from inception to infancy, and one day owning
all the strength that you instilled in him
A man
A king
The Bible says we are gods created in the image of our Heavenly
Father
God in three
The Father, Son, and the Holy Spirit
But still One
You are worthy of every tear that we shed
The pain hurts because the love for you is infinite

We say now and always
We love you
Rest in Perfect Peace
Beloved mother, daughter, sister, lover, cousin, niece, aunty, friend
You are more than these words I'm writing with this pen 🙏

I GIVE MY GRATITUDE AND dedicate this poem "Channa" to my dear
friend Ethlyn Edwards-Marsh for your encouragement, sharing hopes
and dreams with me, and trusting me to write this poem for your beloved
daughter Richanna "Channa Reid" Edwards-Marsh. You dream and
work hard to make those dreams come true for the ones you love to have
a human experience to walk with their heads high and, at the same time,
to be humble and courageous to get back up when they fall. You instilled
that fight and courage in your "baby girl," and she will forever be in
your heart. May the light that she brought into this world continue to
shine bright through each and every one that knew her and loved her!

Sweet Rain Falling!

The rain sounds hard yet sweeter tonight, falling
Through the window, I can feel a breeze
I wish my lover would come calling
I would open my arms wide and give him the tightest squeeze

The rain is falling while the wind is howling
They seem to be doing a magic dance
Sometimes the swishing and then the growling
I will give him a call to come over. I won't leave this night to chance

Such sweet rain
My toes are warm under the blanket
Sleep will come again
Is that his car pulling up and making a racket?

Swaying in the wind, the tallest trees through the window peep
I feel such peace at this moment. I think I'll go back to sleep

Hiding

I know I'm hiding
I'm doing everything except what I'm supposed to be doing
I wake up daily
I ask God to forgive this disobedient child
You've given me tasks to complete
And it seems I'm used to defeat
I procrastinate
I call myself stubborn
And yet you wake me up each morning
And forgive me of my foolishness
I don't know why you chose me
I don't feel worthy
You've sent me help
Angels from above
Angels below
Angels here and now
I could never be
I could never do
All that you have set for me
Without the support
And the help
The guidance
The wisdom
From the shoulders that I stand on
I am humbled
I have stumbled
But I haven't crumbled
I thought I was hiding
I thought I was fearful
But you showed me that you were carrying me

In your arms
Preparing me
Not my time, God
But your will be done
Hide me always
Prepare me always
For I am nothing without you
Today
Tomorrow
And through eternity!

Earth Schooling, Transmute the Pain to Love

Sitting here thinking
I'm glad life showed me all the adversities
It knocked me upside down
I experienced atrocities
Maya, Oprah, Iyanla, Toni, Alice, Nora, Angela, Nikki, bell, V,
    Gloria, Sonia, Audre, Octavia, Viola, Michelle, Shonda,
    Chimamanda, and dem would all agree
We wouldn't trade anything for this journey to be living free
Even though they—we—went through pain thought unforgivable
We lived to see another day
We transmuted that pain to love
We sometimes wished we knew that before we had kids
We don't want to see our sons and daughters hurting
But the pain is there to wake us up
Life is a soul's journey
It's easier to wake up if you are in a nightmare than if you are having a
    nice dream
I heard Eckhart Tolle say
Think of the camel going through the needle's eye
Easier than a rich man who has no time to ponder life
Or the ones who are living in fear that they will disappear
Annihilating others out of fear
Simply because they wish not to die, they will kill even a little child
They will kill others instead of reaching for the sky
We use the fire and burn all the clinging away
It turns out we are the fire, as Baba Ram Dass proclaims
The compassion, empathy, and kindness to live life in the now
No need for running and hiding
We could face the moment

Stay watchful, like the bridegroom is coming
He will come again, this new Earth
It is getting to know your worth
If we could wake up first and live in loving awareness
The souls of our children, we could guide them in love instead of pain
They would not need to hide behind the veil of shame
They could use their human experience to guide other souls
To reach their one goal
To seek the Kingdom of God first
Getting to know themselves
The beautiful light of energy that we all are
We would set the world on fire with compassion
As we all wake up!

Acknowledgments

THIS OPPORTUNITY TO SHARE MY writing with you did not come easy. It is a task that I could not have done alone. Reflecting, I see the connections that have been made and how necessary support is in a person's life.

I first want to thank Alison McBain, who read the first draft, gave her feedback, and took on the task of editing, organizing, illustrating, and supporting me to get it to this final stage of sharing it with you. I thank Alison for her patience, kindness, and excellence!

Secondly, Gabi Coatsworth for creating a space for writers to start their week and offering her knowledge and wisdom to support fellow writers. Cheers to my friend Luther Blackwell, Jr., who asked me to put some poems together for his show. As I was putting all the poems together, I noticed the change in my thoughts and the transformation in my life experiences. I thought to myself, *I have a whole book here*.

I am grateful for the souls in the roles of my children Shantelle, Ace, Kevin, daughter-in-love Roza, and granddaughters Khaia Lee and Amaya Rose for giving me a second chance to build connection in a mother role that fosters love, guidance, empathy, and compassion. My sisters, retired Lt. Col. Pauline "Dawn" Haughton and Lorna "Aletha" Slack, for consciously creating space with me to stay connected. I don't see them often enough but appreciate the connections with cousins Lorna "Maureen Grant" Reno, Beverly Williams Coley, and sister Delise Grant. All my nephews, nieces, cousins are a part of this dream.

Thank you to my childhood friends who embraced me with open arms after decades of missing in action. Cheers to Sheina Harris, Ethlyn Edwards-Marsh, Sheron Freeman, Juliet Reynolds, Jackie Young, Jennieve Amore, Althea Baker Brown, Sonia "Nikki" Elliot, Diana

Crosby, Julie Baker, and Sylvia Baker. Thank you to strangers who became friends just because they simply didn't just watch someone suffering but stepped in, without judgment, as good Samaritans and offered support that truly made a difference. Jim and Bailey are angels that God used at the time when I had settled in and accepted what I learned in society, reaching out for help to a system that told me not to set goals and pursue my dreams but to accept poverty and lacking were all there was for me. The system was labeling me as having an illness that I would likely never overcome and encouraging me to become compliant and reliant on a lifetime of medication. Bailey and Jim's continuous support, patience, and gifts allowed me to take risks and set the course to become captain of my own ship. With many failures, I constantly felt safe enough to fall and get back up because I was not alone.

Thank you to the West Indian American community that believes in the strength of the people. Carolyn Vermont, Lorraine Gibbons, and their sister/friends who learned early and reach back to pave the way for others, especially the younger generation. Thank you to Marsha Gomes-Mckie, founder/director at Caribbean Books Foundation, for supporting a fellow Caribbean writer!

I want to thank Amber Chavous for writing the foreword for me. She shared a story about her grandma on social media. It was a beautiful tribute to her. She is a woman of light and wisdom that transcends through her grandchildren and future generations. It was divine guidance that allowed me to reach out to Amber to write the foreword. Her words describe the journey authentically, and it is always a beautiful thing to be seen, heard, and validated. Her compassion is a gift that encourages me.

Thank you to Kevin P. Chavous, who took the time to write *Voices of Determination: Children That Defy the Odds* to tell the stories of ten children who faced horrific struggles. The kind of support they received through education, and the people who saw them, mattered. I cried through every chapter and reached out to Kevin when I finished reading it. He responded with kindness and compassion to encourage me to keep going.

There are too many people to list for this spiritual journey that shared their stories and let their light shine. I am always grateful for the message on forgiveness shown with Jesus Christ on the cross. Thank you to Oprah Winfrey for her platform of starting Super Soul Sunday, Lifeclass, and Masterclass. Thank you to Ram Dass for using his life as a vehicle to serve!

To the people who supported me during the darkest times of seeking help in a system that couldn't see me, they held hope for me with their unconditional support whether with a kind word or resources. Cheers to Ron Corwin and Beth Blumenthal, who understand that it takes a village and to leave no child behind. Thank you to Rozanne Gates and Suzanne Sheridan for reminding me of my greatness within when I was working to bring my head above the waters. A deep bow to James Mapes for allowing me to pick his brain and gifting me with his book *Quantum Leap Thinking: An Owner's Guide to the Mind*, and his wife Susan Granger for sharing her wisdom and love of movies with me, and asking me the question: do I want to be right or do I want to be happy? Thank you to Sue Wilchinsky, Debbie Angotti, Lynn Laukhuff, Elizabeth Lewis, and so many more of the Greens Farms Academy family that provided a space for my children when I was only wishing and hoping for a better life.

The Bridgeport, Connecticut arts community for creating spaces for writers, artists, poets, and people open to discovering their creativity. Thank you to Frank Borres at American View Productions, Suzanne Kachmar at City Lights Gallery, Shanna T. Melton, The Writer's Group Bridgeport, Reverend Ina Alise Anderson, Emerging Voices Production, Iyaba Ibo Mandingo of iYabarts, Razul Branch at BPT Creates, Bill Derry and Nina Lesiga at PechaKucha Bridgeport, Ernel Grant for his vision of Poetz Realm, and Nikki Nicole Wilson for her free spirit, innovation, and creativity.

Thank you to the staff and leaders at The Westport Library for making it a space for readers, writers, creators, in the community near and far. Alex Giannini and Cody Daigle-Orians introduced me to the Saugatuck StoryFest, where I got to pitch my first book idea and meet writers, too many to list here. Thank you to Kerri Gawreluk and Will Diaz at We Rise Storytelling: Collective, and last but not least, thank you to everyone at Fairfield Scribes for creating a space for authors and poets. Roberto Calas, Founder of the Fairfield Scribes, Edward Ahern, Alison McBain, and all the editors. Cheers!

Support is happening in our daily lives at all times.

Gratitude, even in the darkest times, we shall overcome!

About the Author

MITZY SKY IS AN AWARD-WINNING POET who writes to transmute pain to love. She's consciously unlearning messages that hindered her from living wholeheartedly. Her focus is on letting go of internalized oppression to move from shame to presence, beyond labels. Her joy is learning the power of awareness to have a second chance in this lifetime after experiencing adversities. She enjoys spaces of creativity, traveling, and meeting people but is just as joyful on the couch listening to the rain. Mitzy is included on the Black Movement History Leaders: Past & Present list published in February 2023 by Wildflower Alliance. Her short screenplay *All Mind: The Influencers* placed as a semi-finalist at the 2022 Bridgeport Film Festival, and her poem "Who's the Boss?" received third place in the 2021 CT Press Club Communications Contest. Her poem "In This Moment" was published in *We Are the Change-Makers: Poems Supporting Drop the Disorder,* edited by Jo Watson, and she has been a guest at A Disorder for Everyone! online worldwide festival. She contributed to the anthology *Imagining Monsters*, published by Fairfield Scribes, the Westport Library, and edited by Alison McBain. Her academic paper "Why Beyond the Story?" is included in the 2019 *American Journal for Psychiatric Rehabilitation (AJPR): IRCC Special Issue Boundary Crossings: Systems, Communities, and Expertise,* edited by Larry Davidson, Michael Rowe, Mark Costa, and Chyrell Bellamy at Yale PRCH, and published by the University of Nebraska Press (UNP). She has contributed to the online magazines *The Good Men Project*, *Inner City News*, and *Mad in America*. She developed and facilitated the Compassionate Activism program, where she worked for many years. She created the Beyond the Story© project and is a Blogger/Vlogger at www.mitzysky.com.

Social Media Platforms
Website—MitzySky.com
Linktree—linktr.ee/mitzysky
YouTube—youtube.com/channel/UCq8CVGAmwBhjKLYw2Yetriw
Facebook—facebook.com/MitzySky
Instagram—@Mitzy_Sky
LinkedIn—linkedin.com/in/mitzy-sky-5b902731/
Medium—mitzysky.medium.com/
PechaKucha—pechakucha.com/users/mitzy-sky
Twitter—@MitzySky
Amazon—amazon.com/author/www.mitzysky.com

Made in the USA
Columbia, SC
25 April 2024

34491612R00065